This Book Belongs To:

The Most F✝CKING AWESOME

RUDE & OFFENSIVE

COLORING BOOK

of SWEAR WORDS AND INSULTS

FOR ADULTS ONLY

GO STICK
A CACTUS
UP YOUR ASS!

FUCK
IS ONE
OF MY
FAVORITE
WORDS

I WILL
FUCKING
CUT YOU

I FUCKING
HATE
PEOPLE

FUCK YOU
YOU FUCKING
FUCK

YOU
DIRTY
FUCKING
SLUT

Kiss My
SWEET
SWEET
Ass

CALM YOUR
TITS

SMELLS LIKE
WHORE
IN HERE

THE PERSON
COLORING
THIS PAGE
IS A MASSIVE
CUNT

WHAT'S YOUR
PROBLEM
TINSEL TITS

YOU'RE SO
FUCKING
USELESS
I BET YOU
CAN'T EVEN STAY
IN THE LINES

EAT SHIT
YOU FAT FUCK

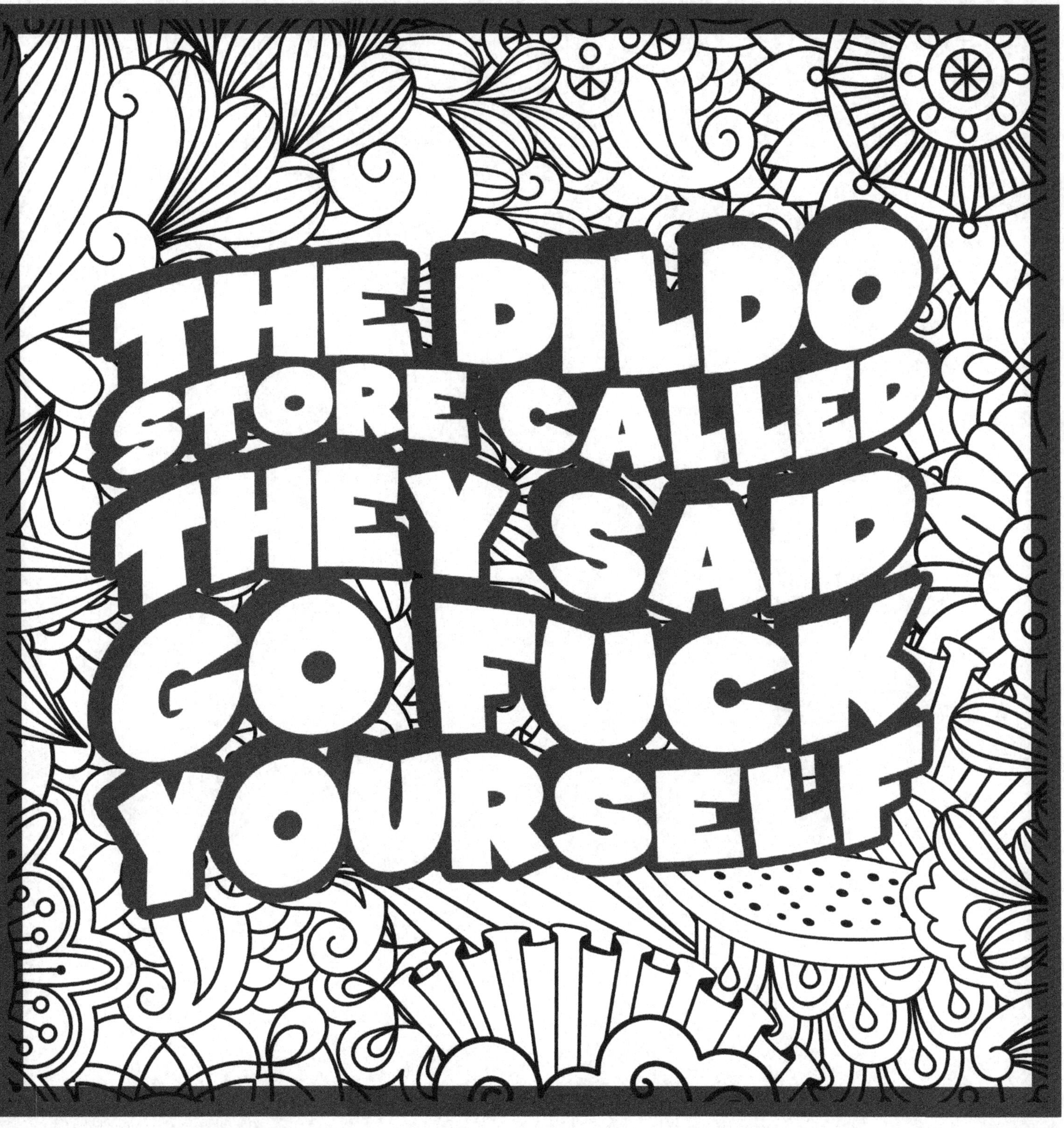
THE DILDO
STORE CALLED
THEY SAID
GO FUCK
YOURSELF

ONCE UPON A TIME
THERE WAS A
TWAT
IT WAS YOU
THE END

FUCK
Fuck
FUCK
Fuck
FUCK
FUCK
FUCK
FUCK
Fuck
FUCK
FUCK
Fuck

LET ME BE
BLUNT
YOU'RE A CUNT

WHAT IN
THE ACTUAL
FUCK

A MESSAGE
TO THE CUNT
COLORING IN
THIS PAGE....
FUCK OFF

FUCK OFF
ON THE HORSE
YOU RODE IN ON

CLASSY
AS
fuck

I'M NOT
ANTI-SOCIAL
I'M PRO
LEAVE ME
THE FUCK
ALONE

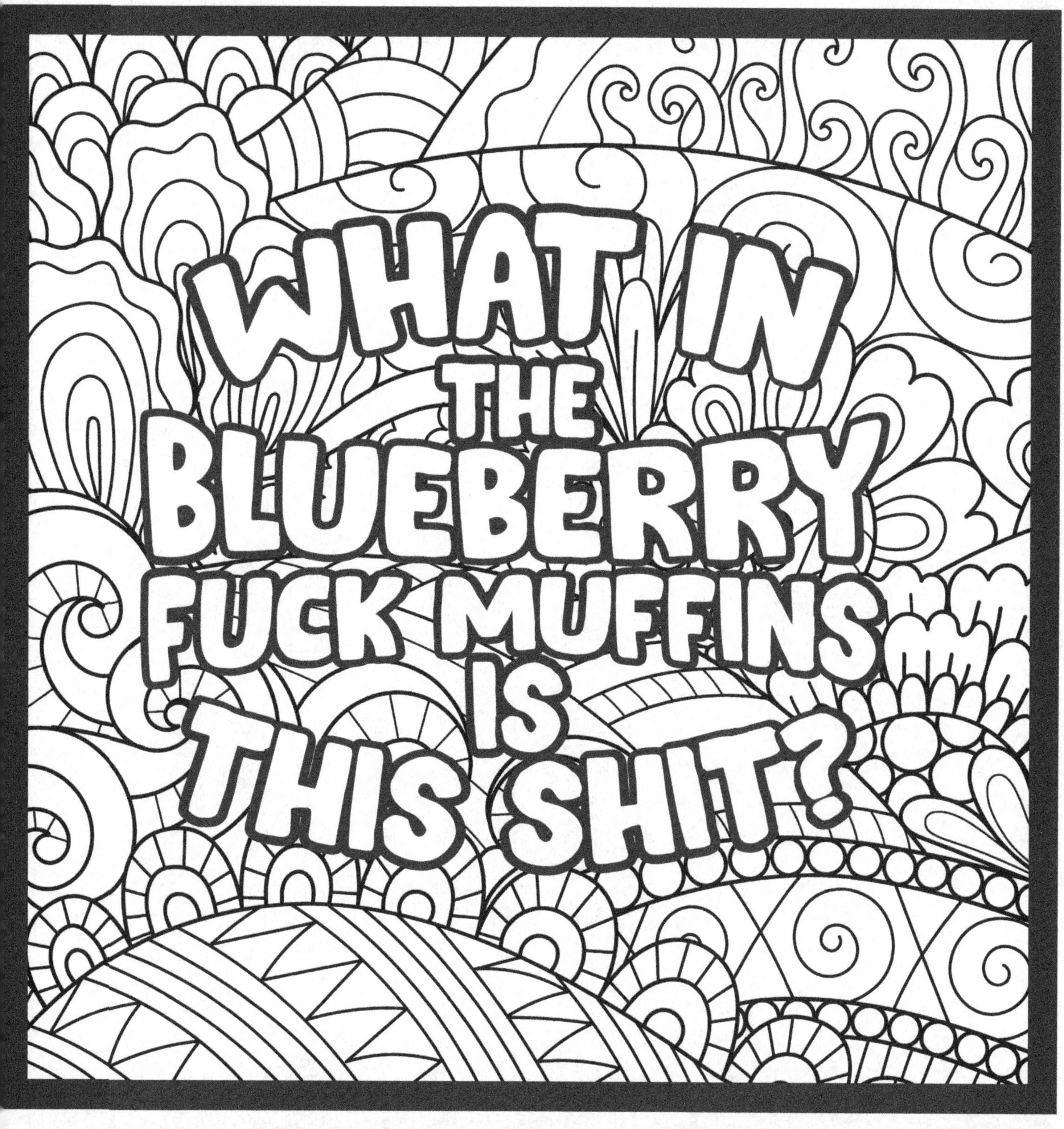
WHAT IN
THE
BLUEBERRY
FUCK MUFFINS
IS
THIS SHIT?

ROSES ARE RED
SHIT IS BROWN
SHUT THE
FUCK UP
AND SIT THE
FUCK DOWN

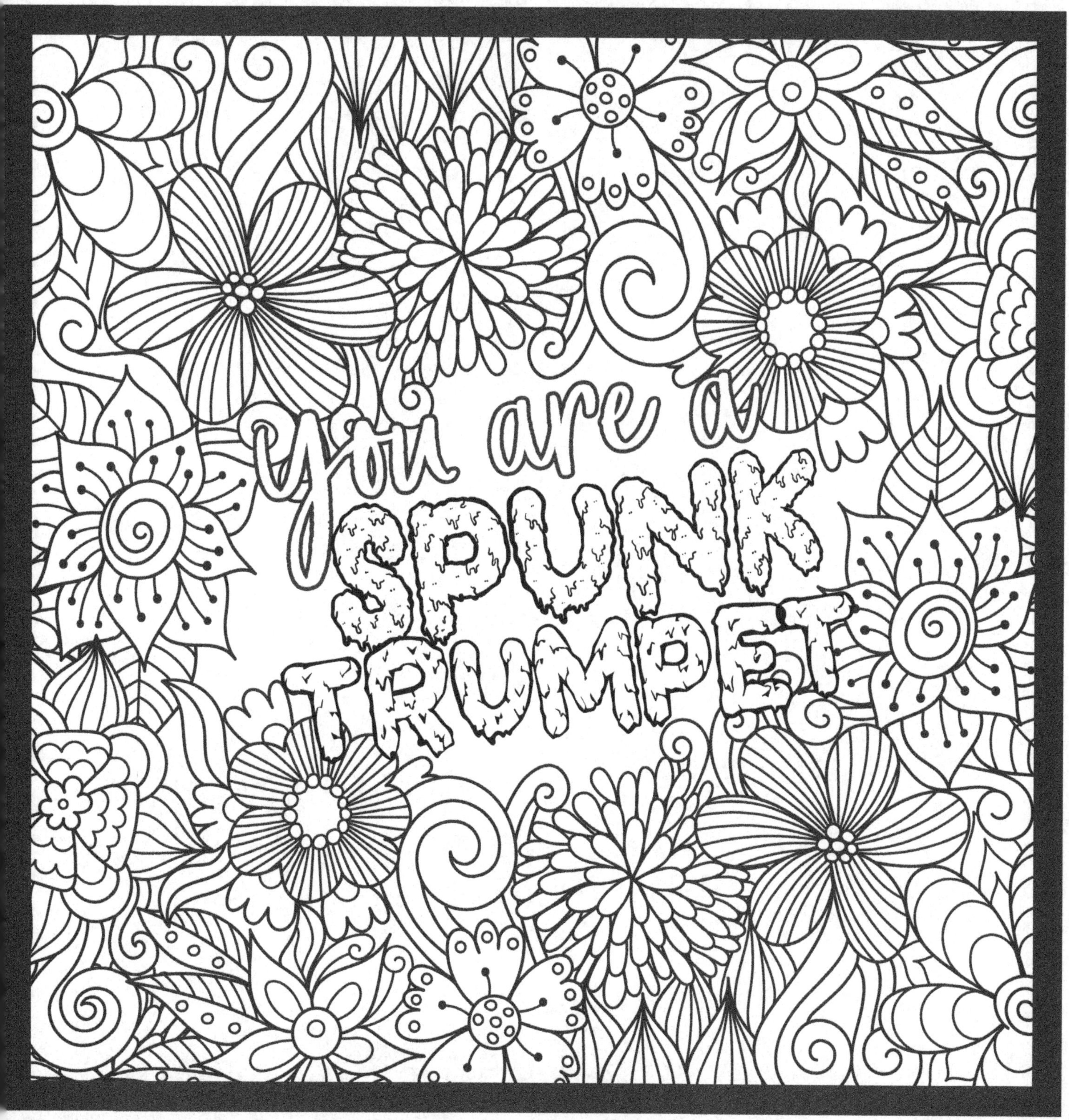
you are a
SPUNK
TRUMPET

THIS IS A
MASSIVE
WASTE OF
FUCKING
SPACE
JUST LIKE
YOU

IN LOVING
MEMORY
OF WHEN
I GAVE A
SHIT

FUCK THIS
FUCK THAT
FUCK OFF
FUCK YOU

WITH A FUCK,
FUCK HERE,
AND A FUCK,
FUCK THERE.
HERE A FUCK,
THERE A FUCK
I DON'T GIVE
A FUCK, FUCK

IF YOU WERE
ANYMORE
OF A FUCKING
BITCH
YOU'D BE HAVING
PUPPIES

Fuck
A
Doodle
Do

I WOULD
SLAP YOU
BUT SHIT
SPLATTERS

Goest &
Fucketh
Thyself

SHUTTING
THE FUCK UP
is also
GLUTEN
FREE

Made in the USA
Las Vegas, NV
24 November 2024

12536494R00039